Construction Industry in Virtual Reality

Reducing Errors and Enhancing Collaboration

Table of Contents

Chapter 1. Introduction

Welcome to this Special Report, where we delve into the fascinating union of the construction industry and virtual reality technology. Entitled "Construction Industry in Virtual Reality: Reducing Errors and Enhancing Collaboration", this report explores the revolutionary shift this synthesis is creating. With our feet firmly planted in comprehensible language and relatable analogies, we aim to benchmark how virtual reality offers a precise, detail-oriented view that aids in significantly decreasing design and construction errors, all while fostering an environment of seamless collaboration. Whether you're a construction veteran, a tech enthusiast, or someone just interested in the way our future cities might be built - this report is an insightful guide into a world where hard hats meet headsets. Dare to envision the construction sites of tomorrow? Well, then this special report is a must-have!

Chapter 2. Introduction to Virtual Reality in Construction

Welcome to the exciting intersection of two disparate fields – the time-tested, concrete world of construction, and the wonderful, elastic universe of virtual reality. You might wonder: How do these two worlds, unalike in so many ways, come together? How do they interact, and what impact do they generate? Well, these are the questions we'll try to address in this section, as we reveal the remarkable shift taking place as these two universes collide and converge.

Virtual reality (VR) is no longer the realm of futuristic fiction or gaming enthusiasts, but a pragmatic tool reinventing the way we design, construct, and experience our built environment. In many respects, VR's journey mirrors the evolution of the construction industry itself, forging new possibilities, building upon the foundation, and shaping the future, one pixel, one brick at a time.

2.1. Understanding Virtual Reality

Virtual reality is an immersive, interactive experience generated by a computer. It's an artificial environment where the user is 'inside' the digital landscape, enabled through VR headsets or multi-projected environments. It creates a genuinely engaging environment that tricks the mind into accepting and experiencing this digital world as a physical reality. Imagine standing in the heart of Rome, experiencing the Sistine Chapel, all from the comfort of your living room.

Virtual reality operates on three primary principles: immersion, interaction, and imagination. Immersion creates a believable environment that absorbs the senses (vision, hearing, feeling), Interaction allows the user to interact and manipulate the virtual environment, and Imagination refers to the possibility of creating any virtual environment as per needs or aspirations.

2.2. VR - A Game-Changer for Construction

While VR technology offers varied applications across industries like education, healthcare, and entertainment, its implications for the construction industry are radical and transformative. They offer potential solutions to some of the construction sector's longstanding problems and inefficiencies.

Importantly, construction projects are typically complex, involving the planning and coordination of numerous tasks and participants. Errors, miscommunication, and misunderstandings can lead to detrimental outcomes, affecting costs, time, and even safety. VR offers a viable and promising solution to these challenges.

Think of VR as a vivid, 3-dimensional blueprint that allows all stakeholders – from architects to engineers, constructors to clients – to step inside their project before a single brick is laid. This approach provides unparalleled clarity and precision, allowing for discussion, review, and amends at the design level itself, hence reducing errors that stem from misinterpretation of 2D blueprints.

2.3. Evolution and Application of VR in Construction

The application of VR in construction is not a recent phenomenon, although the technology's intensity and sophistication have increased multifold over the years. In the early stages, VR primarily facilitated architectural visualization, helping architects and clients visualize the final outcome for improved understanding and decision making. As the technology has matured, its applications encompass every phase of a construction project – design, planning, construction, and maintenance.

In design, VR facilitates real-time immersive experiences of the project. Architects and designers can simulate the space, understand spatial relationships, and effectively accommodate user needs in the design. It empowers clients to walkthrough their projects, experiencing its look and feel, and suggesting changes that fit their vision best.

During the planning and construction phase, VR plays a pivotal role in informing the construction sequence, understanding potential issues, and simulating construction processes. Even after the construction, VR aids in operation and maintenance, providing virtual walkthroughs for training and inspection purposes.

2.4. The Collaborative Edge of VR

A significant advantage of applying VR in construction is its potential to enhance collaboration. Construction is inherently a multi-stakeholder process. Architects, engineers, contractors, and clients - each has a unique perspective, needs, and constraints. Traditionally, coordinating these multiple visions and voices has been a logistical nightmare.

VR offers a shared platform where not only can these stakeholders review and understand the project, but they can do so together - regardless of their geographical location. In a way, it democratizes the design and construction process, allowing all voices to be heard, understood, and integrated.

In conclusion, the application of virtual reality in construction is not just an exciting technological development; it's an essential tool redefining how we approach construction - from planning to the final product. It offers the chance to move away from the inefficiencies and insufficiencies of traditional methods and adopt a more immersive, interactive, and imaginative way of constructing the world around us. The notion of virtual reality in construction is no longer a question of 'if' but 'how quickly' - marking the dawn of a new era in construction.

This comprehensive introduction takes us into a world where the virtual and the concrete meet, a world that's challenging traditional ideas and redefining the parameters of construction. It's the beginning of a fascinating journey into a new era of construction.

Chapter 3. The Technologies Driving VR in Construction

To gain a thorough understanding of how Virtual Reality (VR) integrates with the construction industry, it's imperative to first grasp the technologies that are propelling this novel union. As you navigate through this section, you'll find comprehensive insights on the primary technologies that are helping to drive VR within the construction sector.

3.1. The Nuts and Bolts: VR Hardware

At the heart of Virtual Reality experiences are VR headsets. Also known as "HMDs" or head-mounted displays, these immersive devices vary in capability and form factor, but are unifying in their key function: to transport the user into an interactive, computer-generated environment.

The choice for a VR headset in construction is strongly linked to the type of the project, the complexity of the model, and of course, budget. From high-end systems, such as the Oculus Rift S, HTC Vive Pro, and Varjo XR-3, to more affordable, standalone models, like the Oculus Quest 2, the vividness of the simulation and degree of user interaction can dramatically differ. Regardless of the device, the VR hardware includes trackers, which monitor the user's movements and reproduce them in the virtual world, ensuring an immersive virtual experience.

Beyond the HMD, other equipment may come into play including VR gloves for tactile interaction, and omnidirectional treadmills for unrestricted, natural movement within the virtual space.

3.2. Software Platforms Paving the Way

Hardware is just half the story. Equally critical to a compelling VR experience in construction is the software in use - it shapes the virtual world and sets the parameters for interaction within. The industry largely employs two kinds of VR software: specialized VR platforms for construction and general-purpose VR tools.

Among specialized systems, applications like IrisVR, Unity Reflect, and Enscape are rapidly becoming industry standards. Able to effortlessly integrate with existing architectural designs and engineering tools, these platforms allow professionals to convert BIM (Building Information Models) and CAD (Computer-Aided Design) files into VR environments.

In the realm of general-purpose software, game engines like Unity and Unreal Engine are being co-opted due to their comprehensive toolset for creating high-fidelity, interactive VR experiences. Enabling complex physics simulations, intricate lighting conditions, and lifelike textures, these engines offer next-level realism in architectural visualization.

3.3. Virtual Reality Meet Augmented Reality

Arguably, one of the key driving technologies bolstering VR in construction has its roots in Augmented Reality (AR). Unlike VR, which supplants reality with a virtual one, AR overlays digital information onto the physical world. A blend of the two, known as Mixed Reality (MR), allows users to see and interact with digital content integrated into their real surroundings.

Devices such as Microsoft's HoloLens 2, offer wireless MR

experiences. By scanning the environment and overlaying BIM models onto the real world, they allow practitioners to spot design clashes, analyze construction plans onsite, and evaluate building readiness in real-time.

Chapter 4. Interactivity and User Experience

The effectiveness of VR in construction is heavily reliant on the level of interactivity and ease of user experience it provides. While gaze-based interaction (staring at a point to select it) is a standard method across most HMDs, hand controllers offer much higher interactivity. Advanced systems are now also providing hand tracking, voice commands, and even eye tracking, enriching the user experience and boosting user control within the virtual environment.

4.1. VR and Cloud Computing

The increasing fusion of VR and cloud computing is proving transformative for the construction industry. Cloud platforms like NVIDIA's Omniverse™ allow teams to collaborate and interact with 3D models in real-time. The storage and processing power of the cloud also facilitate handling large design files, advanced rendering, and seamless sharing of virtual experiences, thereby speeding up workflows and democratizing access to VR tools across devices.

To sum up, the integration of VR into the construction domain is underpinned by a diverse suite of hardware devices and software platforms, enriched by advancements in AR and MR, cloud computing, and ever-improving user interaction methods. And even though this description may appear exhaustive, it's only the tip of the iceberg as innovations in the field continue to evolve at an unprecedented rate.

Chapter 5. Minimizing Errors Through Virtual Designs

Errors, particularly in design and construction phases, have a substantial impact on project budgets, timelines, and ultimate success. With traditional methods, such mistakes can be expensive to correct. Virtual Reality (VR) is stepping in as a useful tool to tackle these problems - helping to identify potential pitfalls in the design stage itself and substantially reducing costs associated with late-stage course corrections. Integrating a VR perspective into the construction workflow enables professionals to offer real-time feedback while navigating a 3D environment that simulates the finished structure.

5.1. The Immersive Nature of Virtual Reality

Virtual Reality's ability to create a 3D immersive environment is central to its effectiveness in minimizing errors. By donning VR goggles, architects, construction managers, and clients alike can step 'inside' a building concept long before it begins to take shape in the physical world. This deep-dive exploration allows each detail to be scrutinized and potential design flaws to be identified establishing a vital precursor to the actual construction.

Unlike traditional blueprints and models, VR enables comprehensive, 360-degree exploration of spaces. Users can take virtual walkthroughs moving from room to room, view architectural details from every angle, and even go 'behind' walls to see infrastructure such as wiring or plumbing. This level of detail and spatial awareness far surpasses any traditional, flat schematic, cutting down errors that are often tied to spatial misjudgment or overlooked details.

5.2. Real-Time Feedback and Collaboration

VR's role as a collaborative platform eliminates the segmented process often seen in traditional construction workflows. It makes it possible for architects, engineers, and builders to work together in the same 'room', despite being miles apart geographically. Model iterations are viewable in real-time, meaning that changes made by one party are instantly available to all others.

Furthermore, feedback can be given and incorporated immediately, saving time and reducing the risk of misinterpretations or overlooked communication. For example, an electrician can pinpoint an exact location for an outlet in the VR model, and the architect can instantly make alterations, helping to avoid potential conflicts or interferences with other components.

This early collaborative process results in a more cohesive and informed design, and mitigates the possibility of miscommunications or assumptions that can lead to errors further down the line.

5.3. Enhancing Precision

Precision in architectural design equates to fewer errors during the construction phase. VR tools enhance design precision by incorporating a true-to-scale perspective. Unlike traditional 2D plans, which can lead to misinterpretations of scale, VR models offer a full sense of height, width, depth, and distance between objects. Users can judge distances accurately, enhance layout planning, and anticipate issues like tight spaces or accessibility concerns far earlier in the process.

Additionally, the ability of VR to accurately simulate natural light sources and shadows enables precise planning of windows, skylights, or other light-affecting elements. This reduces the chance of errors related to the purposeful design of light and darkness.

5.4. The Impact of Error Detection on Budget and Time

Construction error rectification is often a strain on both budget and project timelines. Identifying errors in the early phases of design saves not just money but also preserves the integrity of the project schedule.

When errors are caught post-construction, partial or even full demolition may be necessary, leading to waste in materials and labor hours. Additionally, there may be secondary impacts to consider: the cost of delay, potential penalties for late project completion, or the reputational cost of needing to admit and rectify mistakes.

With VR, potential errors are easily identifiable, and the process to correct them is symbiotic with the design process. Changes made in virtual designs do not require additional resources - they simply need a designer's time to adjust the model, avoiding significant cost and timeline overruns.

5.5. Addressing Safety Concerns

Minimizing errors also directly correlates with enhancing worker safety on the construction site. Unexpected anomalies or design mistakes can lead to dangerous working conditions. These could include instability in structures, misplacement of utility lines, or inadequate space for safe movement and operations.

VR technology, with its precise, spatially accurate modeling and predictive capabilities, can detect such safety risks in advance. Mitigation plans can therefore be incorporated into the design before a single brick is laid, making construction sites safer for workers.

In conclusion, VR is revolutionizing the way design and construction errors are minimized. The technology's immersive nature, capacity for real-time collaboration, enhanced precision, cost and time-saving impacts, and concern for worker safety, conclusively make it a game-changer. As we continue harnessing the potential of VR in construction, we can expect to see an industry that better navigates the delicate balance between conceptual design and physical construction.

Chapter 6. Enhanced Collaboration with Interactive Virtual Environments

In a world where global teams and remote methods of working are increasingly common, communication and collaboration have never been more crucial. Evolving further and transcending geographical boundaries, virtual reality (VR) technology is shaping the new age of collaboration in the construction industry. With this tool, teams can work concurrently in a virtual workspace, viewing, interacting with, and modifying the same objects or constructs in real-time, making it an incredibly powerful tool for remote but immersive collaboration.

6.1. Virtual Meetings and Data Visualization

Virtual reality has revolutionized meetings. Instead of sitting around a table with blueprints or looking at computer-aided design (CAD) models on a flat screen, the teams can now meet inside the model. They can virtually immerse themselves and wander around the proposed construction project, inspecting every aspect of the design in great detail.

Graphical data in virtual environments can be manipulated to create immersive data visualization. This ability is an immense advantage in deciphering complex datasets, spatial relationships, volumes, and structures. Collaborators can perceive data in a spatial context far surpassing 2D diagrams and 3D models, making it easier to understand complex constructions, identify issues, and solve problems collaboratively.

6.2. Real-time Design Adjustment and Decision-Making

Virtual reality platforms allow multiple users to interact with each other and also with the 3D model simultaneously. They can add, remove or change aspects of the design, and the changes are seen instantly by all participants. This immediate feedback can tremendously accelerate design cycles by enabling real-time decision-making.

Moreover, changes made in VR can be automatically synchronized with back-end design software in real-time. This function eliminates the need to manually translate or interpret virtual modifications into physical design changes, reducing the risk of data loss or misinterpretation during the process.

6.3. Enhanced Communication and Empathy

Traditionally, interpreting and visualizing project designs from blueprints has been a significant challenge for people not trained in the field. This barrier has often resulted in misunderstandings or miscommunications between stakeholders, leading to costly errors and modifications. By allowing everyone to see, experience, and understand the design in a 3D environment at human scale, VR fosters empathy and shared understanding among various stakeholders, including the ones outside the design team. This common understanding enhances communication and reduces the risk of costly errors due to misinterpretation.

6.4. Training and Safety

Construction sites are inherently hazardous environments, resulting in many accidents despite rigorous safety protocols. VR offers a unique solution to this problem by providing a safe, controlled environment to conduct robust training sessions. Workers can learn how to operate heavy machinery, execute site operations, and respond to emergencies without the risk of real-world consequences.

Through a combination of visual, auditory, and haptic feedback, VR can simulate real-world scenarios with a high degree of accuracy, teaching workers how to navigate and respond to site-specific hazards before they ever set foot on an actual construction site. This immersive training can instill confidence in workers and consequently enhance site safety and productivity.

6.5. The Future of VR and Construction

Looking ahead, the blending of AI with virtual reality can enhance the collaboration further by providing predictive suggestions during design, automating certain functions, or warning against design decisions that violate codes or could create problems down the road.

Gone are the days of simple communicative tools in construction. Today, VR systems offer much more comprehensive and immersive environments to enhance teamwork, promote understanding, rectify design faults, and streamline decision-making processes in real-time. As construction projects evolve into an increasing magnitude of complexity, the adoption of VR technology becomes more of a necessity than a possibility. The benefits echo loudly for enhanced collaboration, improved productivity, and safer construction sites - all leading towards a more sustainable and efficient future for the global construction industry.

Chapter 7. The Evolution of Project Management with VR

Traditionally, project management within the construction industry has been driven by tried and tested manual techniques, but new winds are stirring. The inception of Virtual Reality (VR) in this realm has opened the door to powerful tools and innovative approaches. With VR, the aspirations for accurate planning, enhanced collaboration, error mitigation, and ultimately, cost savings, don't have to remain as mere aspirations.

7.1. The Dawn of Virtual Reality in Construction

VR's entrance into the construction industry did not happen overnight. The evolution of this technology has had its roots in multiple fields, dating back to the 1960s when the first head-mounted display was envisioned. It took many decades from then for VR to gain mainstream acceptance, catalysed by the gaming industry in the early 2010s. Around that same time, astute professionals within the construction industry began experimenting with VR's potential to revolutionize their field.

7.2. VR and Construction Planning

The planning phase, often called the pre-construction phase, is crucial in determining a project's success or failure. It constitutes a meticulous evaluation and mapping of resources, designs, financial implications, and time considerations. Traditionally, this planning phase relied heavily on 2D plans or rudimentary 3D models - a state of affairs that often led to misinterpretations and oversight.

Enter VR. By offering immersive 3D models, VR allows project managers to visualize the complete project, even before any groundwork starts. They can foresee potential design issues, ensure optimal resource allocations, and even effectively plan site logistics. Project stakeholders can walk the virtual site, notice clashes or errors, and wholeheartedly understand the project scope, all within the confines of a virtual environment.

7.3. VR for Design Proofs and Revision

A significant part of project management in construction is communicating and agreeing on the design elements. Often, a non-technical stakeholder might struggle to grasp the implications of a 2D blueprint. This difficulty in understanding frequently gives way to expensive, time-consuming revisions later on.

Here, VR plays a pivotal role. By transforming flat plans into immersive designs, stakeholders become deft at understanding complex architectural elements. They can experience the scale, orientation, space, and function of each area. This experiential understanding facilitates an effective review process, where teams can collectively navigate the design, propose changes, and streamline revisions - without even breaking ground.

7.4. Enhancing Collaboration

Project management in construction has always been a multi-disciplinary affair. In addition to the sheer number of individuals involved, the necessity to align different professionals' expertise and ensure all work towards a common goal poses an array of challenges. The physical separation of teams further accentuates these challenges.

VR offers an antidote to these hurdles, fostering an environment where team members can 'meet' in the same virtual space, despite their geographical locations. This collaborative environment engenders shared understanding and improves decision-making by enforcing a 'single source of truth'. This single source can be explored, discussed and modified by all stakeholders, ensuring that everyone is on the same page.

Furthermore, this virtual collaboration does not have to dilute the human touch. With advancements in VR devices incorporating avatar-representations and hand gestures, meetings in virtual spaces can almost mimic the dynamics of face-to-face sessions.

7.5. Mitigating Errors and Cost Overruns

Errors in construction projects are a constant headache for project managers. These inaccuracies lead to cost overruns, project delays, and a significant waste of resources. These concerns are only exacerbated by the complexity and scale of today's typical construction project.

VR provides a platform for precision and detail, reducing potential design errors and their subsequent consequences. Any clashes, inconsistencies, or omissions in the design can be virtually identified and rectified long before affecting the actual build. This feature has a profound effect on reducing waste, conserving resources, and aiding the industry's push towards sustainability.

7.6. Keeping Up with Schedule

Time is of the essence in construction projects, and delays can be incredibly expensive. Task scheduling and management are key skills possessed by an accomplished project manager. VR technology can assist here, too.

By simulating the stages of construction in a virtual environment, VR can identify potential schedule conflicts, visualize specific tasks related to project phases, and even train teams on intricate procedures before they perform the actual task. The scope for planning and error mitigation is expanded, ultimately leading to smoother project timelines.

7.7. Training and Safety

One of the more subtle benefits of VR in project management is that it can serve as an excellent tool for training and safety. With its realistic representation, VR can create an almost real-world environment where workers can be trained on tasks, handling of machinery, or safety drills. "Practice makes perfect" is the goal here, minus the risk, thereby contributing to reducing accidents on the construction site.

7.8. VR's Future in Construction Project Management

With all its advantages, it seems VR is here to stay within the construction industry. As the cost of this technology continues to decrease and its capabilities increase, its adoption will only grow. The detailed visualizations, enhanced collaboration, error mitigation, schedule optimising, and safety training VR offers presents an enticing prospect for the future of construction project management.

In conclusion, the partnership of construction and VR shows remarkable promise for the future of the industry. While challenges like integration with existing systems, learning curve, and acceptance among more traditional practitioners do exist, the benefits it presents seems to outweigh these limitations. The path forward is clear; VR is set to redefine project management in the construction industry in unprecedented ways.

Whether the construction sector is ready to fully embrace this powerful tool remains to be seen. But all signs point towards an exciting future - a future where VR might just be the beacon leading the way. So, it's time to don those VR headsets, and get building. Virtually!

Chapter 8. Training and Safety: A VR Perspective

The transition of the construction industry into the realm of immersive Virtual Reality (VR) training is not just a trend; it's a paradigm shift. In terms of safety and personnel training, the implementation of VR technologies can create simulated real-world scenarios that are risk-free, cost-effective, immersive, and engagement-focused. It keeps in line with the industry's growing need for better training solutions without sacrificing safety.

8.1. Understanding VR-Based Training

In essence, VR-based training coalesces the real and virtual world, creating an immersive experience for its users. Unlike traditional training methods, VR training plunges participants into a realistically simulated environment, providing a kinesthetic learning approach. This means they can learn by doing, not just observing or listening.

Using high-resolution, stereoscopic headset displays, along with tracking and rendering systems, trainees are able to engage in a vast range of construction-specific scenarios. This includes operating heavy machinery, mastering safety protocols, navigating dangerous sites, and solving complex design issues in a safe, controlled environment. The learners even have the ability to pause, discuss, review, and redo activities without any real-world repercussions.

8.2. The Benefits and Advantages

The value proposition of VR training in the construction industry extends beyond its novelty. It's providing tangible benefits, as listed below, that outweigh traditional training programs on numerous levels.

8.2.1. Improved Safety

By leveraging VR, workers can be trained on safety measures in a simulated environment that mirrors real-life scenarios without the associated risks. For instance, potential dangerous situations like working at heights or maneuvering heavy machinery can be replicated within VR, giving workers hands-on experience without endangering them or others.

8.2.2. Higher Engagement and Retention

Studies have shown that VR training leads to improved retention rates as compared to traditional methods. This is attributed to VR's immersion aspect, where trainees are actively engaged rather than passively learning, leading to increased memory recall.

8.2.3. Cost-Effectiveness

While there is an upfront cost to implementing VR, it may prove more cost-effective over time. Costly on-site accidents can be minimized, and travel costs for multiple training locations are reduced or eliminated. Moreover, VR environments can be reset and reused infinitely, unlike physical training sets.

8.2.4. Real-Time Feedback and Assessment

VR offers a viable platform for real-time feedback and monitoring of a worker's progress. Instructors can assess a trainee's understanding and application of learned skills, allowing for the opportunity to correct mistakes before they become habit.

8.3. VR for Safety Training: A Closer Look

Adopting VR as a tool for safety training comes with its own subset of unique advantages. In a virtual construction site, a worker can virtually "step on a nail," triggering a message about the importance of site cleanliness without any real injury. Likewise, demonstrating the consequences of ignoring safety harness protocols at heights can be simulated realistically, enforcing the importance of such safety measures.

8.3.1. Incident Re-enactment

One effective VR application is the re-enactment of past incidents. By virtually walking through these scenarios, learning points can be extracted and communicated more effectively. It also helps workers understand the real-world implications of not following safety protocols.

8.3.2. Safety Drills

With VR, safety drills like fire evacuation and disaster management can be performed repetitively. This gives workers the opportunity to practice protocols repetitively until they become second nature, ensuring swift, correct actions during an actual disaster.

8.4. Conclusion: The Future of VR-Based Training

The usage of VR in the construction industry has proven to be a transformative force when it comes to training and safety. It offers a differentiated way of equipping construction workers with the knowledge and skills they need to perform their roles, while minimizing the risks associated with traditional training methods.

This doesn't mean VR will replace traditional training methods entirely. Instead, VR can enhance and supplement them, creating a hybrid approach that benefits from the advantages of both. As hardware continues to become more affordable and software more sophisticated, the adoption of VR in the construction industry is a trend we anticipate will grow.

Though still in its nascent stage of integration, VR in the realm of construction training and safety is an exciting prospect to embrace. As developers continue to mold and shape the VR experience to optimize training outcomes, there's a huge potential waiting to be unlocked. Only by embracing this technology can we streamline engagements, uplift training outcomes, and ultimately sculpt safer and more efficient construction sites and personnel - shaping the future of construction.

The journey of integrating VR into the fields of safety and training in the construction industry is just now scaling up. Such is the potential of this revolutionary technology - the future seems to have already arrived. And as we stand on the cusp of this new era, it's clear that innovation is the core building block on which we will construct the future.

Chapter 9. Cost and Time Efficiency Gains in Virtual Construction

Immersing into the sphere where the digital realm meets the physical, where blueprints spring to life before a single brick is laid, and architects, engineers, and project managers collaborate from different regions of the world, we witness how virtual construction garners significant savings in both cost and time.

9.1. The Currency of Virtual Construction: Time and Cost

Virtual Reality (VR) creates a melded environment where project stakeholders can 'walk' through the construction site even before the project commences. By doing so, it allows all parties to identify and rectify any potential structural or design errors in the initial phases, significantly reducing the odds of costly and time-consuming alterations down the line. With such proactive error detection, companies can economize their resources avoiding productivity losses and underrun from surprises that arise from design 'blind spots'.

Liquid Galaxy, for instance, is a multi-screen and immersive experience that was used to virtually navigate the construction of the $4.5 billion Panama Canal extension project. The model facilitated the project stakeholders to identify significant logistical challenges, and the resultant alterations accounted for a saving of nearly 7-10% of the total project cost.

In addition to detecting design errors, VR tools can be used to analyze the efficiency of the proposed construction methods. By simulating different scenarios, project managers can iteratively enhance their strategies until the most time-efficient and cost-effective solution is realized.

9.2. Enhanced Collaborative Planning

In traditional project planning, miscommunications or misunderstandings can lead to costly errors and project delays. However, VR greatly enhances communication and collaboration among the involved parties.

Implementing VR walkthroughs during the planning and design stages holds everyone to the same understanding of the project – nothing 'gets lost in translation'. Architects, designers, engineers, clients, and contractors experience the project from their perspectives, enabling them to provide valuable inputs based on their expertise. This 360-degree collaborative process thus aids in holistic project planning.

Through such collaborative project planning, the risk of unforeseen expenses due to communication mishaps is notably mitigated. Besides, with everyone working with the same understanding, the project is more likely to stay on schedule.

Highmark, a U.S.-based health insurer, was planning to renovate one of its floors. However, instead of traditional methods, they adopted a virtual mock-up. The early-stage projection enabled the employees to understand the layout, offer their feedback which was then incorporated into the design. This process not only promoted staff satisfaction but also saved approximately $700,000.

9.3. Virtual Training: Cutting Training Cost and Downtime

While on-the-job training for construction workers is time-honored, it's also infamously time-intensive and hazardous. Incorporating VR into training regimes simulates practical situations in a controlled and safe environment. It provides a hands-on understanding of the tasks and situations workers might encounter, thus increasing their preparedness.

As compared to in-person training modules, VR training can be undertaken at any time, adding another layer of flexibility and reducing downtime. Moreover, VR eliminates the requirement of expensive equipment or logistics, cementing itself as a cost-effective training method.

9.4. Procurement and Logistics Optimization

VR's benefits extend to the domains of procurement and logistics too. Resource organization done in a virtual platform can minimize misplaced orders and redundancy, keeping cost and schedule overruns in check.

Different project schedules and materials required at various stages can be visualized using VR for easier understanding and management. Systems like these drastically lessen the likelihood of miscommunication, excessive orders, and squandered resources.

9.5. A Move towards Optimal Resource Utilization

A less tangible, yet no less essential, result of embracing VR is optimal utilization of resources - valuable man-hours, materials, and machinery. The precision of VR eliminates 'buffer time' usually added to accommodate unforeseen circumstances, streamlining timelines and efficiencies.

In summary, the surge towards virtual construction demonstrates its prowess in saving time and reducing costs across the industry. As we continue to advance in this digital age, we're not just constructing buildings and cities virtually, but we're also erecting a future replete with cumulative efficiencies of VR. The pairing of construction and technology remains an intriguing intersection set to redefine urban landscapes and redefine our shared experiences of space. As we stand on this brink of transformation, there's no question - VR is constructing a new era in the built environment.

Chapter 10. Case Studies: Successful Implementation of VR in Construction

The novel integration of virtual reality (VR) into the construction industry isn't purely theory, nor experimental hype. It's successful implementation in various real-world projects offers definitive proof of the potential this technology holds, offering solutions to common industry issues and redefining the parameters of design, planning, and collaboration. In this chapter, we'll explore several case studies that highlight VR's defining role in modern construction.

10.1. Beck Group: Voracious Appetite for VR Adaptation

The Beck Group, a multinational architecture and construction company, implemented VR in a bid to improve their architectural visualization process. They used VR to create full-scale, three-dimensional models of their plans, allowing designers, engineers, and clients to virtually tour the proposed structures, identify potential issues and make design tweaks far before construction commenced.

From a design perspective, VR provides an ability to virtually manipulate an environment, encouraging a more intuitive and fluid design process. An interesting case-in-point was the development of Stanley Marketplace, a 22-acre food and shopping center in Colorado. Here, the Beck Group implemented VR to finalize the design. As a result, the client was able to have a fully immersive experience of the space, well before its actual construction, instilling confidence and a clear understanding of the design intent.

The turnkey solutions given by VR saved immense time on the project, virtual site tours reduced ambiguity, and identified mishaps or design flaws early in the process. This case further emphasizes how VR can streamline communication between different stakeholders and significantly reduce errors during construction.

10.2. Mortenson: Advocating for Improved Safety Measures

Mortensen, another player in the construction sector, seized VR to foster better safety protocols at its work sites. Using this technology, they created a 'safety simulation' that accentuates site safety protocols and potential hazards in a virtual ecosystem.

By creating a virtual walk-through of a power plant project in Minnesota, the company could immerse its workers in the simulated site environment. This allowed workers to experience potential safety hazards in a controlled environment. The immersive nature of VR led to increased understanding, retention, and application of safety measures among the construction staff.

Their approach demonstrated that VR can contribute to the construction world outside of design and visualization, emphasizing the technology's potential in training and skill development. Mortensen's approach embodies an added layer of safety to the construction industry—keeping workers well-informed about potential hazards.

10.3. McCarthy: Enhancing the Client Experience

McCarthy Building Companies adopted VR for its client-facing activities. It used this immersive technology to create a 'Virtual Hospitality Suite,' targeting clients in the hospitality sector. The suite offers potential clients a VR tour of their custom-designed sites, which can be viewed either through a VR headset or via a device screen.

By introducing a VR-dependent interaction for their clientele, McCarthy was able to attract more clients. It also aided in strengthening communication and understanding between the firm and its clientele. Clients were no longer limited to imagining the finished construction project through 2D renditions and could instead visualize and experience the complex features of the design virtually.

Virtual walkthroughs also enabled clients to provide accurate feedback on design aspects, leading to an overall better client experience. In this case, VR's utility in bridging the client-contractor gap and facilitating client engagement is well established.

10.4. Bouygues Construction: Collaboration and Training in a Virtual Environment

French construction giant, Bouygues Construction, adopted VR for both collaboration and training. As part of a project to construct a university building in Paris, the company used VR to simulate the construction process, allowing each stakeholder, including the client, subcontractors, and team members, to have virtual tours of the site.

Simultaneously, they adapted VR for staff training. 3D models of their construction sites, coupled with immersive VR experiences, were used to create interactive training sessions. These sessions provided trainees a vivid understanding of the techniques, principles, and safety protocols of their work environment.

Through this approach, Bouygues highlighted how VR empowers construction companies to enhance collaboration between multiple parties and facilitate efficient training methods.

These case studies provide practical insights into how VR's integration in the construction industry redefines traditional practices. They reveal not only the feasibility and versatility of the technology but also the extensive benefits concerning design, safety, collaboration, and client engagement. As VR continues to gain traction in the construction industry, it's customizability, and range of potential applications make it an essential component of future construction and design projects.

Chapter 11. Challenges and Solutions for VR Adoption in Construction

The advent of Virtual Reality (VR) in the construction industry presents an entirely new realm of possibilities, fundamentally transforming the way we conceive, design, and construct our built environment. However, like all new technologies, its adoption is not without its challenges. In this regard, strategizing effective solutions to these issues not only facilitates the successful integration of VR in the construction industry, but also accelerates its benefits for all stakeholders.

11.1. Technological Hurdles

Arguably the most palpable challenges emanate directly from the nature of VR technology itself:

1. **Hardware Issues**: High-quality VR experiences necessitate powerful, often expensive, hardware. Builders also have to decide whether to invest in tethered systems, which are generally more powerful but limit mobility, or untethered systems, which trade a bit of power for portability.

2. **Software Compatibility**: VR solutions need to integrate seamlessly with existing construction industry software. Lack of integration can result in wasted effort and lost productivity.

3. **Tech Savviness**: VR is a technology-intensive tool that requires users to overcome a steep learning curve to fully utilize its capabilities.

The key to overcoming technological hurdles lies in the development of tailored hardware and software solutions for the construction industry. This includes lightweight, affordable, and rugged VR equipment that can withstand the rigors of a construction site. Similarly, the software should emphasize compatibility with existing architecture, engineering and construction (A/E/C) solutions, and user-friendliness to cater to personnel of varying tech literacy levels.

11.2. Cultural Barriers

Resistance to change and skepticism towards new technology can be significant barriers to the adoption of VR in construction.

1. **Risk Aversion**: The construction industry is often risk-averse due to the significant costs associated with errors or delays. Therefore, many firms are hesitant to experiment with new, untested technologies like VR.

2. **Resistance to Change**: In many construction firms, traditional methods are deeply ingrained. Thus, there can be considerable resistance among workers to transition to new technologies, particularly those as radical as VR.

Adopting a progressive company culture is paramount in these scenarios. This includes fostering an environment that encourages technological exploration and proving the tangible benefits of VR through successful project use-cases.

11.3. Health and Safety Issues

VR tools can cause side-effects, such as dizziness or nausea, leading to a phenomenon called "cybersickness." Furthermore, in a construction site, having your vision completely immersed in a virtual world could raise safety issues.

Precautions through the design of VR experiences can mitigate these potential issues. For instance, the VR software should incorporate frequent breaks, static focal points, and gentle movements to reduce the likelihood of cybersickness. As for safety, designated safe zones for VR use on-site and proper supervision can prevent accidents.

11.4. Legal and Privacy Concerns

VR technology raises certain legal and privacy issues. Data collected by VR devices can include sensitive information that could be misused if not properly secured.

To circumvent these issues, companies should implement robust data protection policies that comply with data privacy laws. Additionally, they can also make use of data anonymization techniques to further protect user information.

11.5. Economic Challenges

1. **Cost of Implementation**: The initial cost of investment for both hardware and software can be high, and may deter smaller firms.

2. **Ongoing Maintenance and Updates**: Continual updates and maintenance are often necessary to ensure the VR system's workings are up-to-date, thereby incurring additional expense over time.

To address these challenges, a cost-benefit analysis can be performed - not just on economic terms, but also on the time savings, error reductions, and enhanced collaborative potential that VR offers. In addition, the adoption of pay-per-use or subscription models can also lighten the economic burden on smaller firms.

Though faced with significant challenges, VR possesses the potential to revolutionize the construction industry. By addressing these obstacles head-on and leveraging the power of virtual environments, constructors can not only improve design and project delivery but also enhance their own understanding of the built environment. This journey, albeit with its fair share of hurdles, ushers the industry towards a future where virtual and physical realities coexist.

Chapter 12. The Future of Construction Sites: A VR Preview

The concrete giants we see today are a testament to human innovation in the construction field. The advent of virtual reality (VR) technology is about to revolutionize the processes, efficiencies, and future of construction sites. Admittedly, it might conjure images of video games and sci-fi movies, but the practical implementations of VR are far-reaching and remarkably practical. This chapter takes an exhaustive look into the future of construction sites, a future laden with VR previews, and simulations.

12.1. A New Perspective: Viewing Construction Through VR Lenses

Virtual reality presents a unique angle that's both precise and interactive. Traditionally, blueprint reading has been a complex skill, exclusive to seasoned architects and engineers. With VR, professionals can virtually walk through the entire project even before the first brick is laid. The advent of VR reduces the reliance on the need to interpret 2D plans, altering the way we visualize construction.

Imagine if you could walk around, or even inside, a not-yet-existing building and experience it exactly as you would in the physical world. You can inspect a virtual beam for its exact dimensions or spot design discrepancies. This immersive way of previewing construction sites is quickly shifting from a novelty to a necessity.

12.2. Decimating Margin of Error: Towards Flawless Blueprints

While a structure is imagined in the third dimension, it is translated onto a 2D piece of paper or screen for planning purposes. With VR technology, design and construction teams can now work with 3D models that deliver increased accuracy.

The precise nature of VR can identify areas prone to error and correct them before construction commences. VR models can be analyzed for spatial relationships, accessibility, and other nuances that can be overlooked in conventional plans. This reduces numerous subsequent iterations, saves a lot of rework, and helps avoid expensive errors.

Moreover, VR allows "clash detection" by overlaying various operational systems within the building and spotting the clashes. There's a radical reduction in the trials and errors that exhaust budgets and extend deadlines.

12.3. Enhanced Collaboration: Breaking Constraints of Distance

In the globalized setup, key stakeholders in a construction project might be kilometers apart, operating from different time zones. VR can come to the rescue in such situations and enable a collaborative work environment.

Virtual meeting rooms foster real-time collaboration to review designs and rectify errors. For instance, an architect in New York and an engineer in Berlin can simultaneously walk through a virtual construction site in Tokyo, pointing out modifications, and discussing changes. This environment not only facilitates faster decision-making but also significantly cuts down on travel costs.

12.4. Training and Safety: Prepping For Real-world Challenges

Safety holds paramount importance in the construction industry. VR introduces more effective safety programs by enabling workers to recognize and react to hazardous situations before they encounter them on-site. In essence, VR safety training can cover potentially dangerous scenarios that are too risky to recreate in real life.

Besides safety, these simulations can also aid in skill acquisition for specialized construction tasks. By training in a realistic yet controlled environment, workers can improve their skills while minimizing the risks associated with real-world practice.

12.5. An Eco-friendly Approach

From CO_2 emissions to waste production, the construction industry significantly influences the environment. The integration of VR into the construction world could mitigate these environmental impacts. Through virtual prototyping, problems can be detected earlier, eliminating the need for rework that often leads to material waste. Thus, VR contributes to an overall reduction in the industry's carbon footprint.

In conclusion, the implementation of virtual reality technology into the construction industry is not just the way forward - it's an absolute game-changer. By allowing for thorough inspections, early error detections, seamless collaboration, improved training, and fostering an environmentally friendly approach, VR is priming itself to be fundamental to the future of construction. With this immersive technology, the phenomena of hard hats meeting VR headsets is transforming from unconventional reality to everyday reality.